THE VILE VICTORIANS ACTIVITY BOOK

Terry Deary ✠ Martin Brown

SCHOLASTIC

VILE VICTORIAN QUEEN

Victoria was the queen who ruled Britain between 1837 and 1901. During her reign, she aimed to conquer the world. For such big ideas, Victoria wasn't a big person – she was less than 152cm tall. She made up for it by being about 152cm wide! Funnily enough, this 'shortest' British monarch ruled the 'longest' of any of them.

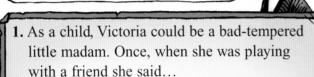

Here's a quick quiz to see how much you know about the chubby little queen.

1. As a child, Victoria could be a bad-tempered little madam. Once, when she was playing with a friend she said…
a) "You must not touch those toys, they are mine, and I may call you Jane, but you must not call me Victoria."
b) "You can play with my toys for as long as you like, and even though I am a princess, you can still call me Vicky."
c) "Take your podgy little fingers off my doll, you vile child."

2. Queen Victoria was afraid of something. Was it:
a) spiders
b) bishops
c) dolls

3. When Victoria's music teacher told her she 'must' practise more, she slammed the piano lid and said,
a) "There! You see, there is no 'must' about it."
b) "Whoops! How clumsy of me."
c) "How dare you tell me what to do. Do you know who I am?"

4. Queen Victoria liked to eat. A cake was named after her – the Victoria Sandwich Cake. What did the royal doctor have to say about the fat queen?
a) "She is on a seafood diet – she sees food and eats it."
b) "She is more like a barrel than anything else."
c) "She must have a belly full of hungry worms."

YOU'RE A BARREL OF LAUGHS

5. When Queen Victoria heard that her husband had died, what did she do?
a) She shrieked one long wild shriek that rang through the horror-stricken castle.
b) She fainted and fell into a deep sleep and didn't wake up for five years.
c) She choked and spat out her false teeth.

6. At Queen Victoria's coronation in 1838, the Archbishop of Canterbury caused her 'great pain'. Did he:
a) drop the imperial state crown with all its 3,250 diamonds on her toe?
b) accidentally prod her in the bottom with the royal sceptre?
c) place the coronation ring on the wrong finger?

YOU CAN GO TO THE PUB NOW

The Victorians enjoyed using the new invention – the camera. They sat very still while their picture was taken … very, very slowly. This is why Victorians rarely smiled in photographs. If the camera 'saw' them move, the image would be blurred. Here are six portraits of vile Queen Victoria. Which one matches the big picture of the queen below?

VILE VICTORIAN CHILDHOOD

You may think your parents are pretty vile. They nag you to tidy your room, force you to eat your spinach and wear sensible clothes. But at least you have some room, some food and some clothes. Many Victorian children weren't that lucky!

"Sticks and stones will break my bones, but names will never hurt me." Oh yeah, who says so? Victorian parents could be cruel to their children in many ways. For example, they could torture them for life by giving them a terrible name. Which of these names were given to Victorian children?

ABISHAG?

FEATHER?

BRAINED?

SHEEPDOG?

HAM?

LETTUCE?

CLAPHAM?

LIZ?

DESPAIR?

TRAM?

KYLIE?

WATER?

ENERGETIC?

WONDERFUL?

MURDER?

Babies are smelly, noisy and expensive to keep. Some parents decided that the best way to deal with this was to get rid of them! Read the 1860's report below. Then find the words in bold in the wordsearch. The words are written forwards, backwards, up, down and diagonally.

O	I	D	C	S		
I	C	Q	U	A	P	G
R	E	Y	S	F	E	U
C	L	A	T	O	T	D
A	L	W	H	I	S	E
N	A	L	O	N	R	R
A	R	I	L	F	O	E
L	S	A	E	A	O	D
S	I	R	S	N	D	R
	C	V	T	E	U	
	F	L	S	A	M	

IN THE LAST FIVE YEARS, IN THIS DISTRICT ALONE, AT LEAST 278 **INFANTS** WERE **MURDERED**; MORE THAN 60 WERE FOUND **DEAD** IN THE THAMES OR THE **CANALS** OR PONDS OF LONDON AND MANY MORE THAN A HUNDRED WERE FOUND DEAD, UNDER **RAILWAY** ARCHES, ON **DOORSTEPS**, IN **DUSTHOLES**, **CELLARS** AND THE LIKE.

Growing up for many children was like getting round an obstacle course of death. Here is a game to see if you would have been one of the lucky ones to survive a vile Victorian childhood. You will need a dice and a playing partner. Take turns rolling the dice and move on the number of spaces shown. The first to reach the end will be rescued by Doctor Barnardo – a man who opened homes for orphan children and educated them, too!

62	61 Run over by a mine truck. Go back to the start.	60	59 Trap your leg in a factory machine. Go back 8 squares.	58	57	56 Lost down the mine. Go back 8 squares.
FINISH						
48	49	50	51	52	53 Climb up a grimy chimney and sweep it clean. Go back 5 squares.	54	55
47	46 Knocked over by a horse and carriage. Go back 6 squares.	45	44	43	42	41	40
32	33	34	35 No food to eat except for a flea-ridden cat. Go back 7 squares.	36	37	38 Drink dirty water and catch a disease. Go back 5 squares.	39
31	30 Smothered by a pillow in your sleep. Go back 5 squares.	29	28	27	26 Trap your arm in a factory machine. Go back 4 squares.	25	24
16	17	18	19 Forced to live in one room with another family. Go back 2 squares.	20	21	22	23
15	14 Sleep in a bed that's filthy with soot. Go back 1 square.	13	12	11	10 Pushed down a coal-hole. Go back 5 squares.	9	8
START	1	2	3 Stand barefoot in the ice selling matches. Go back to the start.	4	5	6	7 Stuck up a chimney. Go back 3 squares.

VILE VICTORIAN LABOUR

When you left Barnardo's at the age of 13, you were placed in a 'Division'. A First Division (top) girl had a good record of conduct and character. She was given a uniform and could get a job as a servant. Fourth Division (bottom) girls were found to be dishonest, violent, vicious and unclean in their personal habits. They would not be sent out to service but were dismissed from Barnardo's or sent to a school of discipline.

DAILY GRIND REMINDER

Here is a typical day of a parlour maid. Read the list of tasks and match each one to the correct picture by drawing a line.

Morning tasks

a) 6.00 a.m.
Yawn! Get out of bed. Wash, dress and brush hair into a bun.

b) 6.30 a.m.
Go downstairs. Put the kettle on. Pull up blinds, open windows, clean fireplaces.

c) 7.00 a.m.
Make early tea; take it to the master and mistress.

d) 7.30 a.m.
Sweep the dining room and dust. Lay the table for breakfast.

e) 8.00 a.m.
Serve breakfast.

f) 8.30 a.m.
Go upstairs, strip the beds, open the bedroom windows, have own breakfast.

g) 9.00 a.m.
Clear breakfast table, wash up, put on clean apron, make the beds, clean the taps, wash the baths and bathroom floors, clean the toilets, dust every bedroom.

h) 12.00 p.m.
Change dress to serve lunch. Lay the lunch table, serve the lunch, clear the table, wash up all the glass and silver, put everything away in its place.

i) 1.00 p.m.
Clean the pantry sink and floor, eat own lunch.

Evening tasks

j) 6.00 p.m.
Lay the table for dinner.

k) 7.00 p.m.
Serve dinner and wait at table.

l) 8.30 p.m.
Clear dinner table, wash up.

m) 10.00 p.m.
Eat own supper, wash up.

n) 10.30 p.m.
Go to bed.

If you were not lucky enough to find work as a servant, you could find other ways to earn your keep. Fancy nail-making or chimney-sweeping? Add the missing words to read about these vile jobs.

Missing words, not in the correct order:
head, sleeping, nail, elbows, ear, knees, fire

Chimney-sweeping

If you think this job was easy, think again! Children often scraped their _____ and _____ as they climbed up inside the chimney. If a worker was found _____ or became stuck in the chimney, his master would light a _____ beneath him.

Nail-making

On average a child would earn three to four shillings a week if his nails were good quality. If not, he could expect a severe beating, or something much worse. One factory worker took a boy and put his _____ down on an iron counter and hammered a _____ through his _____, and the boy made good nails ever since.

YOU GET USED TO IT

Working down the coal mines was a popular career for Victorian children. You were put in a metal cage and plunged down into a mine shaft. Here's the pit where eight year old Geordie works. He's a trapper – someone who opens and closes a heavy trapdoor to let coal wagons pass through. Show Geordie the way out of the mine before he falls asleep on the track!

START

FINISH

VILE VICTORIAN SCHOOLS

So you have to go to school. Blame the Victorians! In 1870 the Education Bill was passed. The aim was to give every child the chance to go to school. But many parents couldn't afford to send their children. It wasn't just the penny a week they had to pay, it was the fact that children didn't have the time to help their mothers with the housework, or earn the family extra money by working.

Some schools had special offers like, 'Three for the price of two.' The parents paid one penny for each of the first two children and the third one got in free. How much would it cost to send thirteen children to school each week?

Some vile Victorian teachers didn't believe in talking to pupils to find out why they did something wrong. They simply punished them. Teachers had a motto … "For bad boys a yard of strap is worth a mile of talk." Can you work out which headmaster is going to use his strap to teach this boy a lesson?

William Shaw was a headmaster at a Victorian school in Yorkshire. He was famous for treating his pupils badly. Shaw was so cruel that two of his pupils lost their sight. Here are six school sins. What punishment would you give each one?

1. Missing Sunday church, punished by…
a) a severe talking-to by the priest and detention while you listen to the sermon you missed
b) a beating with a strap
c) doing extra work for the church – polishing the candlesticks, digging a few graves, copying out of the Bible

2. Throwing ink pellets in class, punished by…
a) a severe talking-to by the teacher
b) kneeling on the floor with your hands behind your head
c) a treble helping of lumpy mashed potato at school dinner

3. Falling asleep in class, punished by…
a) a beating with a metal ruler across the knuckles
b) being hit on the back of the legs with a cane
c) cleaning the floor with your tongue

I WANT TO EAT MY DINNER OFF IT

4. Being late for school, punished by…
a) having your name written in the Punishment Book so you may not get a job when you leave school
b) being hit over the hand with a cane
c) both

SCRIBBLE SCRIBBLE

SWISH

FI

5. Passing notes, punished by…
a) writing the line, 'I must not pass notes in class', a hundred times
b) wearing a 'dunce's cap' and sitting in the corner of the classroom
c) being hit on the bottom with a cane

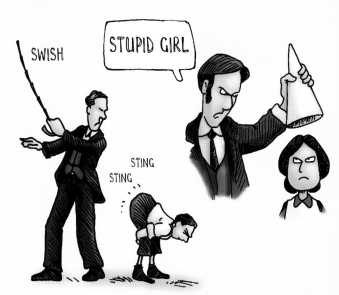

SWISH

STUPID GIRL

STING STING

6. Ink blots and fingermarks on work, punished by…
a) being caned (so your hands are sore and you probably make more mess)
b) having to do the work again
c) death

RIP

After dealing with terrible teachers and painful punishments, Victorian children still found time to play games. Most children had very few toys, unless they made some themselves. They shared toys like hoops, marbles and skipping ropes, with friends in the street, or in the school playground. They also made up games to play, like tag or catch – sound familiar?

Here's a game played by Victorian children in the north-east of England. People from this part of the country are known as "Geordies", hence the game's name. Each competitor has a small ball, or a bean bag if you prefer.

Geordie Bowling

A) Taking turns, throw your ball as far as you can.

B) Collect it and throw it again … and again, until you reach the end of the course.

C) The one who reaches the end with the fewest throws is the winner.

WINNER!

LOSER

In this game, children practised their aiming skills. It's a bit like marbles, but played with buttons or counters.

Up the Buttons

1) Everyone needs a collection of buttons (or counters) to play with. Make sure you can each identify which are your own.

2) Mark a large chalk square on the pavement near the wall of a house (NOT near a road).

3) Mark the word 'OXO' in the centre of the square.

VERY FUNNY

4) Mark a line about one metre from the square.

5) Each player puts their buttons on the line.

6) Take turns to flick each button towards the square (with thumb and finger).

HAND THEM OVER

7) Flick the buttons as many times as you need – but stop when a button enters the square.

8) After all the buttons are in the square, the player whose button is nearest the 'X' of OXO is the winner.

9) The winner gathers up all of the buttons.

Here is a vile Victorian game you must never ever try! Children would tie two door knockers together across the street, rap on the doors, then hide and watch as the two house owners struggled against each other to open the doors! Can you work out which of these strings are tied to which door knockers?

1 2 3 4 5

A B C D E

Only the rich had proper toilets with water to wash the waste into the sewers. The poor had to make do with a small building at the bottom of the yard. There was a wooden bench with a hole in it. Underneath were ashes from a fire. Some vile Victorian children took sticks and dipped them in the waste. They then carried the dirty sticks to the posher streets and wiped them on the door knockers of the houses. Follow the smelly poo sticks and lead the policeman to the fouling offenders.

START

FINISH

POEMS, PLAYS AND SONGS

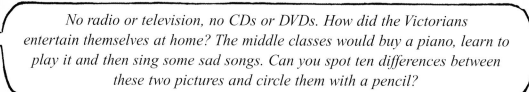

If the Victorians had a favourite subject, then it was death. There was nothing they liked better than a sad story of suffering, heartbreak, tragedy and cruelty. The trouble was it was not just the subjects that were painful. The writing was pretty bad, too! The Victorian ballad writers were probably the world's worst poets.

No radio or television, no CDs or DVDs. How did the Victorians entertain themselves at home? The middle classes would buy a piano, learn to play it and then sing some sad songs. Can you spot ten differences between these two pictures and circle them with a pencil?

Love songs were as popular then as they are today, but can you imagine singing this? Add the missing words to complete this heartbreaking love song. Missing words not in the correct order:

baby   horse
corpse   love
father   pranks
gutter   roar

That is love

See the _____ standing at his cottage door,
Watching the _____ in the _____ rolling o'er,
Laughing at his merry _____, but hark! A _____!
Help! Oh, help him! Gracious Heav'n above!
Dashing down the road there comes a maddened _____!
Out the father rushes with resistless force.
Saves the child… but he lies there,
a mangled _____.
That is love, that is _____!

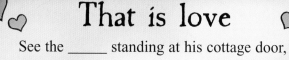

The theatres were very popular. The actors shouted all their lines and made huge gestures with their hands. The plays had simple plots and characters. You booed and hissed the villain and cheered for the hero. Opposite is part of a play called 'Ten Nights in a Bar-Room', written by William W. Pratt. Read the lines and perform it in the street for your neighbours and make a fortune – they'll probably pay you to go away!

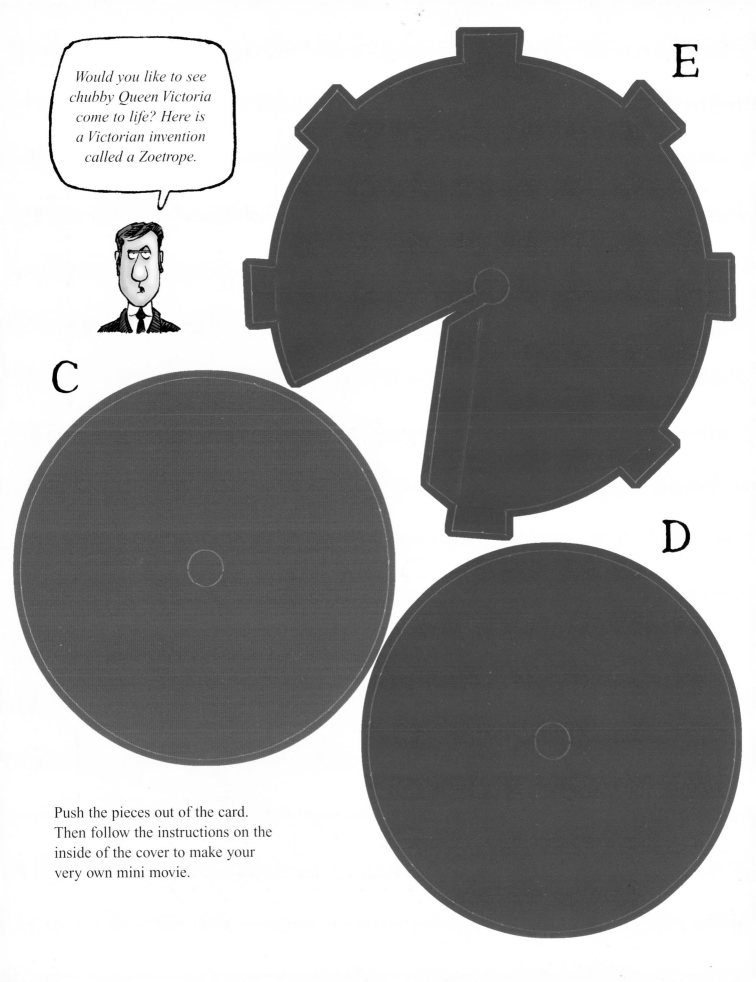

Would you like to see chubby Queen Victoria come to life? Here is a Victorian invention called a Zoetrope.

E

C

D

Push the pieces out of the card. Then follow the instructions on the inside of the cover to make your very own mini movie.

SCENE: Interior of the Sickle and Sheaf Public House. Joe Morgan is drinking with his friends, including Simon Slade, the landlord. Little Mary Morgan is outside the door.

Mary: (Crying) Father! Father! Where is my father? (Enter Mary – she runs to Morgan) Oh! I've found you at last! Now won't you come home with me?

Morgan: Blessings on thee, my little one! Darkly shadowed is the sky that hangs gloomily over thy young head.

Mary: Come, father, mother has been waiting a long time, and I left her crying so sadly. Now do come home and make us all so happy.

Mary: (Singing)
Father, dear father, come home with me now!
The clock in the steeple strikes one.
You promised, dear father, that you would come home
As soon as your day's work was done;
Our fire has gone out – our house is all dark –
And mother's been watching since tea,
With poor brother Benny so sick in her arms,
And no one to help her but me.

Chorus:
Come home, come home, come home,
Please father, dear father, come home.
Hear the sweet voice of the child,
Which the night winds repeat as they roam!
Oh! Who could resist this most plaintive of prayers?
Please, father, dear father, come home.

Father, dear father, come home with me now!
The clock in the steeple strikes two;
The night has grown colder and Benny is worse –
But he has been calling for you.
Indeed he is worse – Ma says he will die,
Perhaps before morning shall dawn;
And this is the message she sent me to bring:
'Come quickly or he will be gone.'

Chorus:
Come home…

Father, dear father, come home with me now!
The clock in the steeple strikes three;
The house is so lonely – the hours are so long
For poor weeping mother and me.
Yes, we are alone – poor Benny is dead,
And gone with the angels of light;
And these were the very last words that he said –
'I want to kiss Papa goodnight!'

Chorus:
Come home…

Morgan: (Suddenly realising the evil of his drinking habit) Yes, my child, I'll go. (Kisses her) You have robbed me of my last penny, Simon Slade, but this treasure still remains. Farewell, friend Slade. (To Mary) Come, dear one, come. I'll go home. Come, come! I'll go, yes, I'll go.
(Exit Morgan and Mary).

VILE VICTORIAN TOWNS

Victorian life was hard and the death rate was very high. Children and their parents worked twelve-hour shifts in the factories and mills. If you were a child, there was a good chance you wouldn't reach the age of 17, due to overwork, lack of food or the poisonous air which was all around you.

Factory life was TIRING, DEADLY, SMOKY, STINKY, POISONOUS, FREEZING, NOISY, STRICT, DIRTY and DANGEROUS. Try and find these words in the wordsearch below. The words are written across, up, down, forwards and backwards.

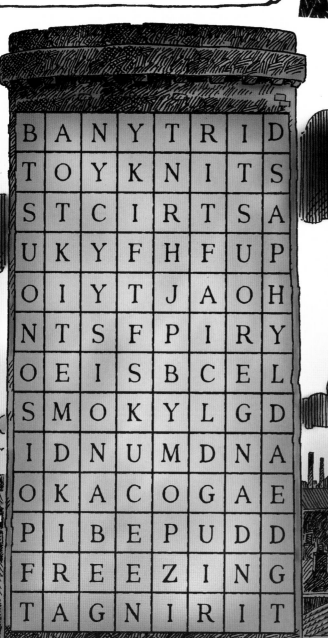

B	A	N	Y	T	R	I	D
T	O	Y	K	N	I	T	S
S	T	C	I	R	T	S	A
U	K	Y	F	H	F	U	P
O	I	Y	T	J	A	O	H
N	T	S	F	P	I	R	Y
O	E	I	S	B	C	E	L
S	M	O	K	Y	L	G	D
I	D	N	U	M	D	N	A
O	K	A	C	O	G	A	E
P	I	B	E	P	U	D	D
F	R	E	E	Z	I	N	G
T	A	G	N	I	R	I	T

Rules for factory workers were as bad as school rules. Which of the following facts were true?

1) There was to be no breathing between 9 a.m. and 5 p.m. True or false?

2) No young children to be brought by parents into the factory. True or false?

3) There was a fine for whistling or singing while you worked. True or false?

4) You started work at 6 a.m. but no breakfast until 8 a.m. True or false?

5) There was a rule against losing fingers in the machinery. True or false?

6) There was a fine for talking with anyone outside your own line of work. True or false?

7) Anyone dying at work would be sacked on the spot. True or false?

VILE VICTORIAN FOOD

If you think your mum's cooking is bad, you should try some of the Victorians' vile recipes – boiled kidneys, soup made from calf's feet, stewed pigeon and a pie made from goose giblets, all washed down with blackberry syrup – anyone feeling hungry?

In 1855, the Sanitary Commission looked closely at the food the Victorians ate and found some interesting things. Unscramble the words to read about some foods that you might think twice about eating.

Starch and flour in ACCOO

Red lead and ochre in cayenne PREPEP

As much as 50 per cent added water in KILM

Insects and fungi in GRUAS

DID YOU ENJOY YOUR LUNCH DEAR?

Copper contamination in preserved TUFIR

Chlorate of lead in STEWES

Alum in DABER (so it would hold water and weigh more)

Frank Buckland, a naturalist, and his father, Dr William Buckland, had a taste for trying unusual food. Read the vile menu below and decide which foods they would and wouldn't have eaten.

Spider eyes – true or false?

Elephant trunk – true or false?

Roast giraffe – true or false?

Boiled nits – true or false?

A mole – true or false?

Stewed bluebottles – true or false?

Alligator – true or false?

Mice on toast – true or false?

Squirrel pie – true or false?

Flea brains – true or false?

Mice in batter – true or false?

Mummified heart of Louis XIV – true or false?

Roast ostrich – true or false?

Monkey toenails – true or false?

COULD YOU PASS ME THE NEWT CHUTNEY PLEASE, FATHER?

Here are two pictures of Frank Buckland and his father tucking into a feast. Can you spot ten differences between them — circle them with a pencil.

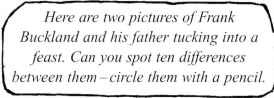

COULD YOU PASS ME THE NEWT CHUTNEY PLEASE, FATHER?

Here is a recipe you might like to try. The Victorians ate it. It won't harm you and you may even like it!

On the other hand, if you want to eat like a poor Victorian, then you might like to try this recipe from Mrs Beeton. She said it was "seasonable at any time, especially during hard times, using whatever ingredients are available."

CANDIED CARROTS

YOU WILL NEED

500g carrots
2 tablespoons golden syrup
2 tablespoons butter
Chopped mint
Salt

1) Use small carrots or larger carrots sliced length-wise. Boil in salted water until tender.
2) Melt the syrup and butter together in a pan.
3) Add the carrots, cook for ten minutes, stirring regularly.
4) Serve sprinkled with chopped mint.
5) Serves four. Ideal with the Sunday roast lamb.

HALF PAY PUDDING

YOU WILL NEED

250g suet
125g breadcrumbs
250g flour
A handful of currants and raisins
2 tablespoons treacle
Half pint of milk (minimum)

1) Put the suet and flour in a mixing bowl and rub in thoroughly.
2) Add raisins and currants, and mix.
3) Slowly add the milk, stirring continuously until the mixture is thick and smooth.
4) Add treacle and stir well.
5) Place in a greased, oven-proof bowl and gently sprinkle breadcrumbs on the top.
6) Cook in a moderate oven until risen and breadcrumbs become toasted.
7) Serves all the family — but the more there are the less you get!

17

VILE VICTORIAN ARMY

Queen Victoria had an army that invaded other countries. They would take the wealth and the natural resources from each country (diamonds from South Africa, sugar from the West Indies and so on). Queen Victoria was very proud of her army. The army was pretty proud of itself. And that's surprising because they weren't very good.

Solve the picture clues and fill in the answers in the grid. The numbers in brackets show the number of letters in each answer.

(7)

(5)

(6)

(5)

(4)

(5)

(7)

(5)

W A R

U

O

When you have filled in the right answers, you will be able to add the word (in the blue column) to complete this fact: The Brits had the world's largest empire during the reign of Queen Victoria—they _____ over a quarter of the globe!

Draw a picture of a brave British soldier. Copy the lines in each square onto the empty grid. Then colour your picture in. Soldiers wore red uniform jackets—this made them easy targets—but at least they didn't show the blood.

Florence Nightingale became a legend for her nursing work during the Crimean war in Russia. In 1854, she visited the hospitals in Scutari. Add the missing words to read about the terrible conditions...

1) The men can lie in _____ for two weeks before being seen by a doctor.
2) The floors are crawling with _____ and insects.
3) Operations are carried out in the _____ in full view of everyone.
4) The _____ of the men having _____ cut off is terrible.
5) There are 1000 men in one hospital, many with _____.

6) The _____ overflow onto the floor.
7) Men without _____ or slippers must paddle through this.
8) Amputated limbs are dumped outside to be eaten by _____.

Missing words, not in the correct order: diarrhoea, dogs, filth, limbs, screams, shoes, toilets, vermin, ward.

Here are two pictures that show the terrible conditions that were reported by Florence Nightingale. Find ten differences between the two and circle them with a pencil.

VILE VICTORIAN VILLAINS

The Victorian villains would cut your throat, poison you, club you to death or shoot you just for the sake of your purse. As if these thieves and murderers weren't bad enough in real life, the Victorians made up even worse horrors in their books. Count Dracula, Sweeney Todd and Doctor Jekyll and Mr Hyde were all Victorian inventions.

Jack the Ripper was a real live villain who killed up to eight women. He became a legend as the vilest Victorian of them all, but was never caught. Here are eight silhouettes of the dreaded murderer. Which one matches the silhouette lurking in the dark alley.

1   2   3   4

I THINK IT'S NUMBER 7

5   6   7   8

Victorians thought they could tell a criminal by his looks and general appearance. Things they looked for were:

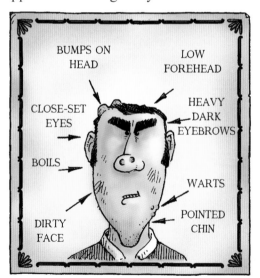

BUMPS ON HEAD

LOW FOREHEAD

CLOSE-SET EYES

HEAVY DARK EYEBROWS

BOILS

WARTS

DIRTY FACE

POINTED CHIN

… and anyone who was shifty or acted suspiciously. Most of the population were like this really! Using the characteristics above, try and draw your own ugly Victorian criminal!

WANTED

If the vilest criminal is the one who murders the most, then Britain's worst killer murdered four times as many victims as Jack the Ripper. In July 1872, in West Auckland, County Durham, an inquest was held into the death of a little boy, Charles Edward Cotton. Here is the evidence. What do you think the jury decided?

GUILTY OR NOT GUILTY?

YOU ARE ACCUSING MARY-ANN COTTON OF MURDER — WHY?

I OFFERED HER A NURSING JOB AND THIS IS WHAT HAPPENED...

I CAN'T WORK WHILE I HAVE THE BOY, CAN'T YOU PUT HIM IN THE WORKHOUSE?

YOU'LL HAVE TO GO, TOO

NEVER MIND, HE'LL PROBABLY GO LIKE THE REST OF THE COTTON FAMILY

YOU MEAN THIS HEALTHY LITTLE FELLOW IS GOING TO DIE?

YOU'LL SEE HE'LL NOT GROW UP

THEN ON FRIDAY SHE WAS STANDING IN HER DOORWAY AND SHE SAID TO ME...

THE BOY'S DEAD

DOCTOR KILBURN CAME AND EXAMINED THE BODY

CALL DOCTOR KILBURN!

I HAD BEEN TREATING THE BOY FOR AN UPSET STOMACH. I GAVE HIM MORPHIA FOR THE PAIN AND HYDROCYANIC ACID FOR THE FEVER

ISN'T HYDROCYANIC ACID A POISON?

IT WAS A VERY WEAK MIXTURE YOUR HONOUR

AND WHEN YOU EXAMINED THE CONTENTS OF THE BOY'S STOMACH?

THERE WAS A WHITE POWDER THERE — THE STOMACH WAS INFLAMED

COULD THE WHITE POWDER HAVE BEEN POISON?

IT COULD — OR IT COULD HAVE BEEN THE MORPHINE I GAVE HIM

AND THE INFLAMMATION? POISON?

OR THE BOY'S ILLNESS. I HAVEN'T HAD TIME TO TEST IT

CALL MRS MARY-ANN COTTON

I GAVE MY STEP-SON ARROWROOT — AND I BOUGHT THE ARROWROOT FROM RILEY THERE! HE HATES ME BECAUSE I WON'T GO OUT WITH HIM!

ASK HER ABOUT HER HUSBAND'S DEATH, AND HER OTHER THREE CHILDREN WHO DIED SINCE SHE ARRIVED HERE!

SILENCE IN COURT! THE JURY MUST FORGET THEY EVER HEARD THAT REMARK. NOW, JURY, YOU DECIDE. DID CHARLES EDWARD DIE OF POISONING? IF SO, WHO POISONED HIM AND WAS IT DELIBERATE OR ACCIDENTAL? OR DID CHARLES EDWARD DIE NATURALLY OF A STOMACH FEVER?

VILE VICTORIAN QUIZ

So you think you know a thing or two about the vile Victorians? Test your knowledge with this multiple choice quiz and see if you're a true Victorian expert or not.

1. A Victorian husband had the legal right to…
a) lock up his wife
b) beat his wife
c) own all his wife's belongings, clothes and money

WHAT'S HERS IS MINE

2. Who wrote the dreadful lines of poetry, describing a pond:
I've measured it from side to side;
'Tis three feet long and two feet wide.?
a) famous Victorian poet, W S Gilbert, in the 'Pirates of Penzance'
b) famous Victorian poet, William Wordsworth
c) Queen Victoria in her diaries

3. Who died in 1870 claiming they were 'exhausted by fame'.?
a) Charles Dickens
b) Lewis Carroll
c) Queen Victoria

4. If you were a working-class Victorian what was the average age you could expect to live?
a) 37 years   **b)** 27 years   **c)** 17 years

LIFE'S NOT SO BAD SON… IF THEY DON'T WORK YER TOO MUCH, AND A MACHINE DON'T KILL YER, AND YER DON'T STARVE, AND YER DON'T GET POISONED, OR FROZEN, OR DISEASED, OR SACKED, OR CRIPPLED…

5) How old was the youngest chimney-sweep in 1804?
a. nine years old
b. four years old
c. ten years old

6. Robert Peel (1788-1850) was famous for what?
a) bringing the first oranges into the country – that's where we get the phrase 'orange peel'
b) founding the first police force – that's why they were called 'Peelers'
c) being the first man to swim the English Channel blindfolded

7. Queen Victoria's son-in-law, Prince Christian, lost an eye in a shooting accident. At dinner parties he entertained guests with his collection of…
a) guns
b) glass eyes
c) stuffed animals

THIS IS MY BLACK EYE

8. Victorians thought it was rude to use the word 'leg'. Instead they used the word…
a) unmentionable – as in, 'We are having a lamb's unmentionable for Sunday lunch.'
b) limb – as in, 'He's only pulling your limb, Jim.'
c) that-which-you walk-on – as in, 'You put your right that-which-you walk-on in, you put your left that which-you-walk-on out, in out, in out, shake it all about.'

MY POOR POOR HUSBAND TRIPPED OVER THE UNMENTIONABLE OF THE CHAIR, HURT HIS THAT-WHICH-YOU-WALK-ON, AND PUT A RIP IN HIS SOUTHERN NECESSITIES

ANSWER PAGES

PAGES 2-3: VILE VICTORIAN QUEEN

Here's a quick quiz to see...

1 = a   2 = b   3 = a   4 = b   5 = a   6 = c

The Victorians enjoyed using...

Portrait F matches.

PAGES 4-5: VILE VICTORIAN CHILDHOOD

You may think your parents are...

All are vile Victorian names except Kylie and Sheepdog.

Babies are smelly, noisy and expensive...

	O	I	D	C	S	
I	C	Q	U	A	P	G
R	E	Y	S	F	E	U
C	L	A	T	O	T	D
A	L	W	H	I	S	E
N	A	L	O	N	R	R
A	R	I	L	F	O	E
L	S	A	E	A	O	D
S	I	R	S	N	D	R
	C	V	T	E	U	
	F	L	S	A	M	

PAGES 6-7: VILE VICTORIAN LABOUR

Here is a typical day of...

A = 5   B = 2   C = 4   D = 11   E = 8   F = 3
G = 13   H = 9   I = 10   J = 12   K = 1   L = 6
M = 7   N = 14

If you were not lucky enough to find work...

Missing words in the correct order: elbows, knees, sleeping, fire, head, nail, ear.

Working down the coal mines...

PAGES 8-9: VILE VICTORIAN SCHOOLS

Some schools had special offers...

It would cost 9 pennies.

Some vile Victorian teachers...

Headmaster C is going to use his strap.

William Shaw was a headmaster...

1 = b   2 = b   3 = a   4 = c   5 = b   6 = a

PAGES 10-11: VICTORIAN FUN AND GAMES

Here is a vile Victorian game...

1 = D   2 = A   3 = E   4 = B   5 = C

Only the rich had proper toilets with water...

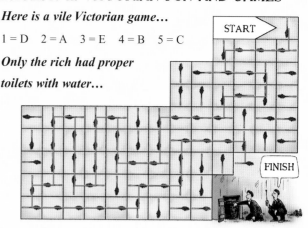

PAGES 12-13: POEMS, PLAYS AND SONGS

No radio or television, no CDs or DVDs...

Love songs were as popular then...

Missing words in the correct order: father, baby, gutter, pranks, roar, horse, corpse, love.

PAGES 14-15: VILE VICTORIAN TOWNS

Factory life was...

B	A	N	Y	T	R	I	D
T	O	Y	K	N	I	T	S
S	T	C	I	R	T	S	A
U	K	Y	F	H	F	U	P
O	I	Y	T	J	A	O	H
N	T	S	F	P	I	R	Y
O	E	I	S	B	C	E	L
S	M	O	K	Y	L	G	D
I	D	N	U	M	D	N	A
O	K	A	C	O	G	A	E
P	I	B	E	P	U	D	D
F	R	E	E	Z	I	N	G
T	A	G	N	I	R	I	T

Rules for factory workers were…

1 = False   2 = False   3 = True   4 = True   5 = False
6 = True   7 = False

Poor workers shared their houses…

PAGES 16-17: VILE VICTORIAN FOOD

In 1855, the Sanitary Commission…

• As much as 50 per cent added water in MILK
• Starch and flour in COCOA
• Red lead and ochre in cayenne PEPPER
• Insects and fungi in SUGAR
• Copper contamination in preserved FRUIT
• Alum in BREAD (so it would hold water and weigh more)
• Chlorate of lead in SWEETS

Frank Buckland, a naturalist…

They ate all of the menu apart from spider eyes, boiled nits, flea brains and monkey toenails.

Here are two pictures of Frank Buckland…

PAGES 18-19: VILE VICTORIAN ARMY

Solve the picture clues…

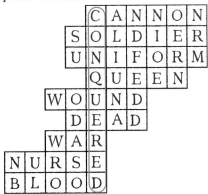

Florence Nightingale became…

Missing words in the correct order: filth, vermin, ward, screams, limbs, diarrhoea, toilets, shoes, dogs.

Here are two pictures that show…

PAGES 20-21: VILE VICTORIAN VILLAINS

Jack the Ripper was a real live villain…

Number 4 is the correct silhouette.

If the vilest criminal is the one who…

The jury decided that Charles Edward died naturally of a stomach fever. Mary-Ann Cotton was free. Then the local newspapers checked her past life and found she had moved around the North of England and lost three husbands, a lover, a friend, her mother and at least a dozen children. And they had all died of stomach fevers! The doctor tested the white powder in Charles Edward's stomach. It was the deadly poison, arsenic. Mary-Ann Cotton was tried for murder, found guilty and hanged at Durham Jail in 1873.

PAGE 22: VILE VICTORIAN QUIZ

So you think you know a thing…

1 = c   2 = a   3 = a   4 = c   5 = b   6 = b   7 = b   8 = b

Scholastic Children's Books,
Commonwealth House, 1–19 New Oxford Street,
London WC1A 1NU, UK
A division of Scholastic Ltd
London ~ New York ~ Toronto ~ Auckland ~
Sydney ~ Mexico City ~ New Delhi ~ Hong Kong
Published in the UK by Scholastic Ltd, 2004
Some of the material in this book has previously
been published in Horrible Histories:
The Vile Victorians and *Cruel Crime and
Painful Punishment*

Text copyright © Terry Deary, 1994, 2002
Illustrations copyright © Martin Brown, 1994–2002
All rights reserved

ISBN 0 439 96296 X

2 4 6 8 10 9 7 5 3

The right of Terry Deary and Martin Brown to be
identified as the author and illustrator of this work
respectively has been asserted by them in
accordance with the Copyright, Designs and
Patents Act, 1988.

Additional material by John Malam
Additional illustrations and colour work by
Stuart Martin

Created and produced by The Complete Works,
St Mary's Road, Royal Leamington Spa,
Warwickshire CV31 1JP, UK

Printed and bound
by Tien Wah Press Pte. Ltd, Singapore